DISCARD

02/02

Children of
SLOVAKIA

THE WORLD'S CHILDREN

Children of
SLOVAKIA

SHEILA KINKADE
PHOTOGRAPHS BY ELAINE LITTLE

Carolrhoda Books, Inc./Minneapolis

We are grateful to the Children of Slovakia Foundation for introducing us to the many programs and people that are making a positive and lasting difference in young lives throughout Slovakia. —E. L. & S. K.

The publisher wishes to thank Ms. Marta Murarova for her generous assistance in the preparation of this book.

Carolrhoda Books, Inc.
A division of Lerner Publishing Group
241 First Avenue North
Minneapolis, MN 55401 U.S.A.

Website address: www.lernerbooks.com

LIBRARY OF CONGRESS CATALOGING-IN-PUBLICATION DATA

Kinkade, Sheila, 1962–
    Children of Slovakia / by Sheila Kinkade; photographs by Elaine Little.
       p.   cm. — (The world's children)
    Includes index.
    Summary: Introduces the history, geography, and culture of Slovakia through the daily lives of children who live there.
    ISBN 1-57505-446-9 (lib. bdg. : alk. paper)
    1. Slovakia—Social life and customs—Juvenile literature. 2. Children—Slovakia—Juvenile literature. [1. Slovakia—Social life and customs.] I. Little, Elaine, 1958– ill. II. Title. III. World's children (Minneapolis, Minn.)
DB2847 .K56 2001
943.7305—dc21   99-050944

Manufactured in the United States of America
1 2 3 4 5 6 – JR – 06 05 04 03 02 01

Church bells are ringing in Bratislava, the capital city of Slovakia. That means it's noon. Adriana and her grandmother take a moment to rest on a bench in the city's Main Square. The square is a popular place to watch people, eat, hear concerts, shop, or just sit and relax. This part of town is just for people—no cars are allowed on the narrow streets leading to the square.

Most of the nearby buildings were built more than 400 years ago. For centuries, Slovaks young and old have come to the square to shop, to be entertained, and to hear the day's news.

Above: *Adriana*. Left: *Young people hanging out in Bratislava's Main Square*

Slovakia is a small country located in the heart of central Europe. About 5.4 million people live there. The country covers about 18,923 square miles. That makes it slightly larger than the states of New Hampshire and Vermont combined.

Slovakia is also a new country. After centuries of being part of other nations or empires, Slovakia became its own country in 1993. Since then, its economy has undergone great change, as it has been opened to trade with western countries.

Bratislava Castle overlooks the Danube River, which passes through the capital city of Bratislava. For hundreds of years, boats and barges on the Danube have transported people, food, and raw materials across Europe.

Atop the highest hill in Bratislava sits a huge *hrad*, or castle, known as Bratislava Castle. The first people to live in the area known as Slovakia settled on this hill more than 6,000 years ago. The hill overlooks the Danube River, one of Europe's major waterways. The Danube stretches for 1,777 miles from Germany all the way to the Black Sea in eastern Europe.

Over the years, different groups of people settled in Slovakia. Around 1000 B.C., a Celtic group known as the Boii came from northern parts of Europe. They established an active trading community in the area. Later, in the A.D. 500s, people known as Slavs began settling in central Europe. The Slavic groups in the western part of the region included Czechs and Slovaks.

Around A.D. 1000, much of central Europe was taken over by the Hungarian Empire. Trade along the Danube River made Slovakia a valuable area. Over the next 900 years, different groups battled for control of Slovakia, but it stayed mostly under Hungarian rule.

A group of students explores the area around Bratislava Castle. It was first built in the A.D. 800s and was destroyed and rebuilt several times over the next few centuries.

Hungarian rule of Slovakia came to an end after World War I (1914–1918). In 1918 Czechs and Slovaks created a new and independent state known as Czechoslovakia. Soon after World War II (1939–1945), Communist leaders gained power in Czechoslovakia and other central and eastern European countries. Czechoslovakia was declared a Communist country in 1948.

While shopping with his mother in Bratislava, Tomas stops to play on a bronze statue. It represents Slovak soldiers who fought from ditches during World War II.

While Slovakia was allied with Germany, many Slovaks rebelled and fought against Germany. Tomas likes the way the statue looks like it grows right out of the sidewalk.

Under Communism, the government took control of farms, factories, and industry. People were not allowed to voice their opinions in the press or to criticize the government. Despite the government's efforts to modernize Czechoslovakia, its economy grew weaker. People became more and more discontent with the Communist leadership.

In the city of Bratislava, modern concrete buildings stand near churches and homes that are centuries old. St. Martin's Cathedral was built in the 1400s.

By the late 1980s, protests became stronger and more open. Finally, in 1989 the Communist government was forced out and a new government was formed. Soon after, Czechs and Slovaks began to disagree about how the country should be run. In 1992, the country's leaders peacefully decided to split Czechoslovakia into two states, the Czech Republic and Slovakia. Slovakia became officially independent in early 1993.

Above: *Young Slovaks play at a McDonald's restaurant in Bratislava.* Left: *Tomas checks out a statue of a Slovak soldier who fought against the German army in World War II.*

11

Marek and Stevo

Since the end of Communism, young Slovaks have seen many changes in their country. Marek and Stevo are excited to be growing up during this time. With the opening of the Slovak economy, the boys' surroundings have become more colorful. Advertising signs and posters from other countries decorate streets and shops. Many Slovak ads also use designs inspired by western companies.

Under Communism, few products from other countries were available in Slovakia, and most people could not afford them. These days, stores sell TVs, radios, VCRs, sneakers, sports equipment, and other products made in Europe, Asia, and the United States. Bookstores sell more books. Toy stores carry a greater variety of toys. While these items can be expensive, more people have the money to buy them.

Marek and Stevo enjoy watching new TV shows and movies from other countries. They like going to fast-food restaurants and shopping for clothes. Both boys' parents are not as sure about the changes. While they welcome new opportunities, many parents worry that traditions of the past will be lost. Marek says his parents talk to him about not putting too much emphasis on buying. He agrees with them, but he still enjoys shopping.

Slovaks of all ages enjoy the products from western countries that have become available to them since the fall of Communism in 1989.

The Bratislava Children's Choir performs songs in five different languages.

Despite recent changes, singing remains a cherished tradition in Slovakia. Twice a week, the Bratislava Children's Choir gathers to practice. Tonight, they will sing songs from around the world before an audience at the Bishop's Palace. Choir members have learned to sing songs in five languages: German, Japanese, English, Czech, and Slovak, the national language of Slovakia.

Near Bratislava's Main Square, Maria and her friends perform in a children's music festival. They belong to a group that meets once a week to practice singing and dancing. They also pray and study the Bible, the holy book of the Christian religion. Most Slovaks are Christians and most practice the Roman Catholic faith.

Maria is 12 years old and loves to sing and perform before audiences. She and the other girls attend a *skola,* or school, nearby. Like some Slovak schools, it is run by the Catholic Church. Most schools are run by the government. Slovak children begin school at age three, when they attend a preschool, or *materska skola.* At age six they begin the *zakladna skola,* or elementary school, which they attend for eight years. Some students continue on to secondary school.

Maria (third from left) performs with her music group near the Main Square of Bratislava.

Maria arrives at school promptly at 8:00 in the morning. She and her classmates begin the day with a prayer, often led by Sister Miriam, the school's headmistress. Sister Miriam also teaches religion, which is Maria's favorite class. Maria also attends classes in math, biology, geography, history, music, and the Slovak language.

Most Slovak students also study a foreign language.

Above: *Maria in class.* Right: *Maria (lower right) and her classmates surround Sister Miriam (center) outside their school.*

They can choose English, French, or German. Most young people in Slovakia speak some English. Many learn English words by watching American movies and television shows, or by listening to music on the radio.

All students also attend a physical education class in the afternoon. In the fall, the boys play soccer, Slovakia's most popular team sport. The girls play a game called *vybijana*. Divided into two teams, the girls throw a rubber ball at members of the other team. If a player is hit, she must step out of the game. When all the members of a team are out, the other team wins.

Above: *Boys play soccer on the playground at Maria's school.* Left: *Maria and her classmates play* vybijana.

17

Michael lives just outside Bratislava with his family. For his twelfth birthday, his father took Michael and four friends to a McDonald's restaurant for lunch. For the boys, going to McDonald's is a real treat. There are not many McDonald's restaurants in Slovakia, and they cost more than other casual restaurants.

Afterward, they went to an amusement park. Michael's sister Ivana also came along with her friend Dagmara. The boys enjoy driving into each other in bumper cars and racing around the track in go-carts. Ivana and Dagmara prefer the Ferris wheel. All of the children have fun running up and down the halls of the house of mirrors, trying to find their way out.

Ivana will turn 12 next year. She has already asked her parents if she can have a party at McDonald's and a trip to the amusement park with her friends.

Michael celebrates his twelfth birthday with his family and friends.

Left: *Michael's sister Ivana waits for a ride on the Ferris wheel.* Above: *Ivana and her friend Dagmara try out the bumper cars.*

Above: *Roman and Juraj play chess at a youth center near their apartment complex.* Right: *Petrzalka is made up of many buildings like this one.*

Roman and Juraj live in a large area of Bratislava known as Petrzalka. Petrzalka is made up of many tall apartment buildings built close together. On sunny days, colorful bands of laundry hang from the buildings' balconies. During the 1950s, Slovakia's Communist government built many such housing projects for the growing numbers of people moving to cities.

Roman shares a bedroom with his older brother. His family's apartment is like most of the apartments in Petrzalka. It has two bedrooms, a living room, a kitchen, and a bathroom. In Petrzalka, there are only a few grassy areas where children can play. Every afternoon, Roman and his friends go to a youth center. There they play ping-pong, pool, table hockey, chess, and other games.

Above: *Roman plays pool at the youth center.* Left: *Laundry and flowers decorate the balconies of Petrzalka apartments.*

Roman's parents both have good jobs. Other families are not as fortunate. Since the early 1990s, Slovakia's economy has been improving, but many people still have trouble finding jobs. The average Slovak worker earns about $182 a month. Roman works hard at school and wants to go to college. He hopes that his education will help him find a good job when he's older.

Anna Maria, Paula, and Adriana are getting ready to go hiking. Every Saturday, they travel with about 50 other young people from Petrzalka to a camp called Kon-Ti-Ki, north of Bratislava. The camp is located at the base of the Little Carpathian Mountains, which are part of the large Carpathian mountain range.

Children at Kon-Ti-Ki sleep in bunk beds in small cabins. Early each morning, everyone sits in a circle around an open fire to warm up and drink hot soup. Most nights, everyone gathers before a big bonfire to sing and tell stories.

On this day, Jakub is planning to play baseball in the afternoon. Later, he'll perform in a play with Hana, Marek, and Juraj. All the campers look up to Milan, the leader of Kon-Ti-Ki. Milan's nickname is *Klokan*, which means "kangaroo," because he likes to wear a jacket with a big pocket in the front.

Anna Maria, Paula, and Adriana

Jakub (bottom row center) and other campers get ready for a baseball game.

"*Ahoy,*" or "hello," Katka says as she arrives at the theater. Katka lives in the small town of Pezinok in western Slovakia. She is 17 years old and is studying to be a teacher.

One or two afternoons each week, Katka rehearses plays with children and adults with mental or physical disabilities. At first she was nervous about working with the other cast members. But after a short while, Katka felt comfortable with her new friends, and she enjoys being with them. She hopes that the group and its performances will help others better understand and accept people with disabilities.

Left: *Katka practices her role in "The Rehearsal Place."* Above: *Katka with Viera, the theater's director*

The group is working on a play called "The Rehearsal Place." It's about a musician who is secretly directing a play about the people of a small town. Tonight is opening night, and Katka expects that about a hundred people will attend.

Peter is 16 and a natural actor. He plays a mayor who is frustrated because all the townspeople keep asking him for favors. Viera, the director, encourages Peter and the other actors to perform with lots of emotion.

Viera directs Peter (far left) and other actors on stage.

25

More than half of Slovakia's citizens live in cities, and the rest live in small villages and rural areas. About 10 percent of Slovaks make their living by farming. Slovak families grow corn, potatoes, beets, and other vegetables. Others raise animals such as cows, pigs, sheep, goats, and chickens.

Farmland is scarce in northern Slovakia, where small mountain ranges are separated by lakes and forested river valleys. Still, many Slovak families manage to farm small plots of land near their homes.

Slovakia has many natural resources, including coal, iron, and timber. Almost half of all Slovaks have jobs in manufacturing and industry.

Top and bottom: *In Cicmany, mothers and grandmothers take young Slovaks for a stroll. The town is known for its uniquely decorated buildings.*

In the 1950s, the Communist government built many factories to produce machinery, steel, and weapons for sale to other countries.

Waste from factories and growing cities has polluted many of Slovakia's rivers and streams. In addition, chemicals released from factories mix with water droplets in the air to form acid rain. When acid rain falls, it does great damage to trees and other plants. Like other European countries, Slovakia is trying to find ways to address the problems of pollution without hurting its economy.

Below: Slovakia's countryside is dotted with small villages like this one, near the Low Tatras mountains. Right: *This coal-burning power plant in the town of Novaky contributes to Slovakia's pollution problem.*

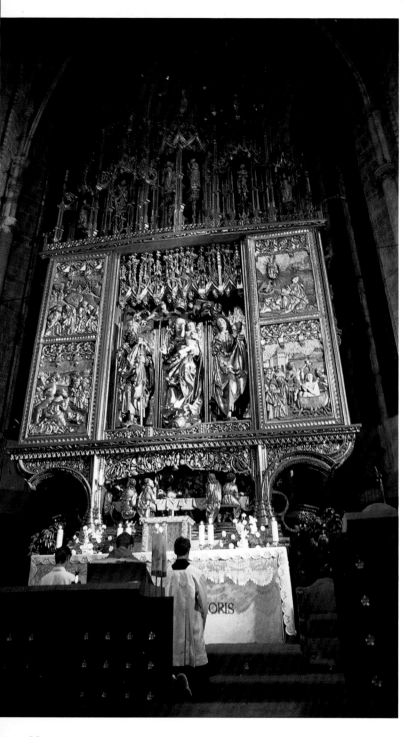

Left: *The main altar at St. Jacob's Cathedral stands over 50 feet high.*
Above: *Daniela and Michal pray at a smaller altar.*

Daniela and Michal live in Levoca, a city in northeastern Slovakia. On Sunday nights, they attend Catholic mass with their mother and father at St. Jacob's Cathedral. Built nearly 600 years ago, St. Jacob's is famous for its beautiful carved wooden altar.

During mass, Michal and Daniela listen while the priest reads from the Bible. They look forward to singing holy songs, or hymns, with the rest of the congregation. After mass, they kneel to pray before a small altar in the church.

Slovakia's Communist government forbade the open practice of religion, and many churches were closed. But since the end of Communism, worship has again become an important part of many Slovaks' lives. All over the country, there are many beautiful, old churches. One of the most famous churches is St. Martin's Cathedral in Bratislava.

Most Slovaks follow the Roman Catholic faith, but some belong to other Christian groups. Slovakia also has a small Jewish community.

Left: *St. Elizabeth's Cathedral in Kosice.* Above: *Most villages in Slovakia are centered around a small church, like this one in Cicmany.*

The courtyard of the children's home in Necpaly

In the middle of the village of Necpaly stands a large house called a children's home, or orphanage. More than 60 children live there. About 10,000 young Slovaks live in children's homes. Many children come to live in a home because their parents have died or become too sick to care for them. In other cases, children have come to the home because they were treated badly. At the Necpaly home, children have a safe place to live, regular meals, a school, and adults who care for them.

Monika is 11 years old. She and the other children get up at 6:30 in the morning on school days and go to bed at 9:00 at night. The children share bedrooms, with five or six children in each room. Older children help younger ones, and everyone does chores like washing dishes or taking clothes to the laundry.

Above: *Marcel does a somersault on his bed. He and his sister came to the home after their father died.* Left: *Monika likes to draw characters from her favorite movies. She has hung a large drawing of Pocahontas over her bed.*

31

Children enjoy their big Sunday meal.

Every Sunday, children at the Necpaly home enjoy a special big meal in the middle of the day. Everybody waits in line for a steaming bowl of chicken soup with long, thin noodles. Then they fill their plates with cabbage salad, beef rolled in bread crumbs and fried, and white rice.

Jozka and Jarka are best friends. They share a room with three other girls. During their free time, both girls like to watch television with other friends. They also like to sing and dance to popular songs on the radio.

Most of the children are sad when they arrive at the home, but over time it becomes a different kind of family for them. They may still get lonely and miss being part of a family. But they become close friends with the other children and the adults who care for them. They must live by strict rules, but they also enjoy learning how to live together.

Above right: *Watching TV at the Necpaly home.* Right: *Best friends Jozka and Jarka*

The village of Chminianske Jakubovany in eastern Slovakia

The village of Chminianske Jakubovany lies in eastern Slovakia. Most people living in the village are part of the ethnic group known as Romanies. Also known as Gypsies, Romanies make up about 1.5 percent of Slovakia's population.

Romanies first came to the area known as Slovakia in the 1400s. They traveled from place to place in caravans, collecting scraps of metal and making them into cups, buckets, and metal baskets. In modern times, most Romanies no longer move from place to place. Instead, most live together in villages or on the outskirts of towns. Romanies are often treated as outsiders, and most are very poor.

Valika is 11 and attends school in Chminianske Jakubovany. Her school is especially for Romany children. Most Romany children grow up speaking only the Romany language at home. They learn Slovak at school. They also study math, science, history, and religion. Most Romanies follow the Catholic faith.

Left: *Valika.* Above: *While their teacher plays the guitar, Romany schoolchildren learn songs in both the Romany and Slovak languages.*

Just outside the city of Prievidza, Sandra and her friends skip rope during recess. Their school is just a short walk away from Bojnice Castle, one of the most beautiful castles in Slovakia. For Sandra and other young Slovaks, visiting a castle is a great way to learn about their country's history. They can actually see the place where noblemen and noblewomen and their servants lived hundreds of years ago. Slovaks also study castles in school and hear stories handed down for generations. Some of Slovakia's castles are in ruins, but many have been preserved.

Left: *Sandra plays at recess.* Above: *Built more than 800 years ago, Bojnice Castle is surrounded by a deep ditch called a moat. The moat was once filled with water to keep enemy soldiers from reaching the castle walls.*

Trencin Castle towers above the surrounding area. It once belonged to Matus Cak, a powerful Slovak nobleman.

Beckov Castle stands high on a rocky cliff. Not much remains of the structure that was built more than 700 years ago. According to legend, a prince built it for his favorite clown. The wall surrounding the castle is carved with U-shapes. The open spaces are known as crenels, and the solid upright pieces are called merlons. Long ago, guards protecting the castle hid behind the merlons and shot arrows through the crenels.

"Dobry den," or "good day," Jana says as she walks into Mrs. Zilincarova's shop. Mrs. Zilincarova owns a pottery shop in Modra, a small town near Bratislava. Modra is famous for its pottery and its wine. The town is surrounded by wineries, or farms where grapes are grown to produce wine. Some families in Modra even grow grapes in their backyard.

Jana has come to the shop looking for a birthday gift for her mother. She carefully looks through the shelves, which are filled with plates, pitchers, vases, and Christmas ornaments.

Making traditional folk art is still a popular activity in Slovakia, and shops like Mrs. Zilincarova's are found throughout the country. In Bratislava, artists and craftspeople display handmade jewelry, baskets, wooden toys, and puppets along the Main Square. Marta searches for just the right necklace to buy for her best friend. Marta likes shopping in stores, but the crafts sold on the street cost less. They are also special because they are handmade.

Marta looks for a special present in the Main Square in Bratislava.

Anna and her family are visiting her grandparents in the small town of Stupava. In general, Slovak families are very close and spend lots of time together. Anna's whole family sits around the kitchen table as her grandmother serves homemade apple *strudla*. A flaky pastry, *strudla* is a traditional Slovak dessert.

Above: Anna's great-grandmother reads to Anna (left) and her cousins. Right: The whole family sits down for some homemade apple strudla.

Anna's sister, mother, and great-grandmother look at old family photographs and tell stories.

Anna's mother, whom she calls *Mami,* works for an organization that helps children in Slovakia. Her father, whom she calls *Tato,* is an architect. He works on restoring and preserving historic buildings.

Anna calls her great-grandmother *Starenka. Starenka* lives with Anna's grandmother, and she enjoys reading to Anna and her brothers and sisters. She also tells the children stories about when she was growing up in Slovakia and about how life has changed over the years.

41

As she tries on a traditional costume, Anna is very careful with the delicate lace trim.

Later in the day, friends come for dinner, and Anna tries on a traditional Slovak costume that has been in her family for more than a hundred years. Anna's grandmother keeps the costume carefully folded and wrapped in plastic behind her bed. She takes it out only on special occasions.

Many years ago, these outfits were worn for religious events and celebrations. Anna's great-grandmother wore the skirt on her wedding day in 1929. Anna has worn the outfit only once, to a church celebration in the nearby village of Marianka. Each year, thousands of people make a sacred journey, or pilgrimage, to the church in Marianka.

The embroidery on Anna's costume was sewn by hand. Each region of Slovakia has its own traditional design. In the region where Anna lives, blue and white thread is usually used. Anna knows a little about doing embroidery, but very few Slovaks continue this tradition. Most clothes are now sewn by machines. Anna's grandmother says the new designs are not nearly as nice.

When it's time for Anna to leave, she kisses her grand-parents and great-grand-mother goodnight. Anna and her sister and brothers are growing up in a time of great change in Slovakia. Through school, television, and movies, young Slovaks like Anna are being exposed to life in other parts of the world.

Yet Anna also remains con-nected to her country and its rich past. Through the stories of parents and grand-parents, young Slovaks learn what it was like to grow up in Slovakia many years ago. Anna's father teaches her about the history found in Slovakia's old buildings and the importance of preserv-ing them. Through her mother's work, Anna learns about the problems faced by other children in Slovakia.

Like Anna, young Slovaks have many opportunities that their parents and grandparents did not have. Even as they remember the past and keep Slovak traditions alive, they face the future with enthusiasm and hope.

Pronunciation Guide

ahoy ah-HOH-ee
Bojnice boy-neet-zeh
Bratislava brah-tih-SLAH-vuh
Chminianske Jakubovany KHEEM-nee-
  ahn-skuh YAH-koo-buh-vah-nee
Cicmany CHICH-muh-nee
Czechoslovakia chek-oh-sloh-VAH-kee-uh
Danube DAN-yoob
dobry den doh-BREE dehn
hrad hrahd
Klokan KLOH-kahn
Levoca luh-voh-chuh
Mami mah-MEE
Necpaly NETZ-pah-lee
Petrzalka pet-ruh-ZHAHL-kuh
Prievidza PREE-eh-vee-tzuh
skola SHKOH-lah
Slovakia sloh-VAH-kee-uh
Starenka STAH-reng-kuh
strudla SHTROOD-luh
Tato TAH-toh
vybijana vee-BEE-yah-nah

Index